THOUGHTS IN MY MIND

SOMYA JAIN

Made with ♥ on the Notion Press Platform
www.notionpress.com

Contents

Contents

Acknowledgements

I would like to thank my parents,
Mr Sandeep Jain and Mrs Reena Jain
for their unwavering support and love on every poem I have written so far!

Prologue

This book is a short collection of a few poems I have written over the years.

The book is divided into four sections to capture the general essence of each work.

1. WHIMPERS OF MIND

The poems in this section are works written primarily in moments where I have ended up thinking about myself, where I have been clouded by mists of self-doubt, pondering about how quickly the sand of time is slipping through my hands.
A lot of times when I sit back and reflect, I end up overthinking and the storm of thoughts that pass through my head at 1000km/hr get collected on paper in a few words that I am able to trap for microseconds.
I wish often times that I don't procrastinate as much as I do, that way I would have more content to present to you Dear Reader, but alas, life is 90% wishing and 10% working for me. So with this I present to you the first section, Whimpers of Mind.

Mess

Sitting here at my desk,
As my imagination blooms,
I feel like a mess...
Waiting for something-
Wishing it was a little different...
That life was as easy as it seemed to be!

How did I grow up?
When will I grow up?
My dreams are tailing me,
They need a fuel,
Anxiety has it, it's burning my soul away...
Can you live sans a soul too?

I live like a zombie...
Crawling through the day,
Fighting like a soldier,
A never ending battle-
A war against myself!
My procrastination making me stumble every now and then!

Thoughts are morphing into overthinking...
Does the cycle ever stop?
Ideas flow, pessimism is my blood-

Questioning everything is all that I do now...
What should I do, is there someone who can help?

Trying to achieve is my new hobby...
Destiny is the bus I am waiting to catch!
Will it take me to my dreamland?
Happiness, joy, ecstaticly overwhelmed: the feelings I wish I would feel someday!

The Stark Realization

In the wake of tomorrow, I have suddenly realized,
It was only yesterday, that I was a child!

Small and innocent, I had no worries,
I was free from all of life's miseries.

As I sit back and reflect, today I am just a year before eighteen,
And have realized, life is not the Eden garden I had dreamed!

Obstacles, hurdles and draughts cover my goals,
Whenever I am in to play a major role!

Life is such an irony one wonders,

Today the living is told:
'you act like a dead man!'

And the dead are told:
'may you get a good life in heaven'

On one hand, I am told 'God helps in times of trouble'

And on the other 'God helps only those who help themselves'

Now will someone help me?

It is said that whatever happens never fear!

Be brave, think about your goals and cheer!

The light will shine and the clouds will clear!

Rain only comes where there is a lot of heat,

So as long as you are determined there is nothing you can't beat!

Waiting

Heart-beating,
Stomach-fluttering,
Eyes watering,
Hands shaking,
Why is waiting so knackering?

Every minute equals an hour,
Every thought sends a tremor,
Every cell in the body is anxious,
Every body is making me nervous,
Why is waiting so arduous?

Will the end be happy?
Or will it make me cry?
Will the story be a memory?
Or will it be something to bury deep inside?
Why is waiting so gruelling?

All's well that ends well,
But will I be able to survive?
Only time will stay to tell my story,
Once I say goodbye!
Why is waiting so mysterious?

Pain

Sadness and despair tear my heart,
Little salty beads dripping down my cheeks,
A thought in my mind making me question: is everything going as I want it to be?

Days pass and grief grows,
A shiver running through my spine making me feel cold,
My mind is weary and my feelings a stone on my chest,
How will these days ever pass I wonder, will I ever feel happiness again?

Working day and night, I chase the little light of hope,
My body aching from exhaustion,
My eyes closing on their own,
My will shaking with every blow,
My confidence ripped to shreds as I plough,
How will I survive if I do, where do souls like mine seek penance?

Time

I was busy, waiting for time to still;
Writing assignments, attending classes, studying with all my will!

I was busy, waiting for time to still;
Travelling new places, making memories that last to my heart's fill!

I was busy, waiting for time to still;
Unaware of how it was running from in between my finger tips!

Time is still now and the atmosphere covered with nothing but tranquility;
But how I miss the mayhem and bedlam that made my life hyphy!

I like to work is what I have concluded;
Or is it the idea of it that makes me feel complete?

2. MOMENTS OF HOPE

Phew! The previous section was heavy or was it? In this section, let me take you through some works that were written in moments where I aimed to motivate, where I wanted to feel empowered or wanted to express emotions that I have not necessarily felt before. As someone who spends her time drowned in the lands of fiction, I don't really always live in reality and that stems buds of feelings that I want to express outloud but don't have an audience for. With this, I present to you the second section, Moments of Hope and I take the liberty to assume that you will come out motivated at the end of this section.

Unconquerable

I was trying to climb a summit,
I fell again and again
Didn't give up, started again,
But did I reach there?

When I fell the 100th time, I lost all hope,
All I could see was my failure,
Clouds of despair brought about a monsoon of tears!

I cried incessantly till my nose was red and my eyes puffy,
All I could feel was sad!
Nothing in this world could make me feel happy again?

I started again, void of any emotions,
Like a coded machinery, climbed up till my rusted parts could no longer function!

Looking up to curse my luck, I saw only the sky,
Where did the peak disappear, my mind boggled in broad daylight!

Suddenly a realisation struck,
And I couldn't handle the emotional burst
I was there my mind screamed but,
I still felt numb,

My inner consciousness mocked my achievement,
You could have done it sooner it repeated like a mantra!

Confidence burnt to ashes,
I now climbed down with my head hanging low,
Flashes of camera bringing me back to reality,
'Congratulations on being the first person to scale this peak!'

We Met Face To Face

The way your eyes shine when you smile,
The way they twitch when you are riled!

The way we talk long hours after class,
The way you can see right through me as if I were glass!

I can't stay without seeing your face,
Would it be the same had we met at a virtual place?

Dream

Men are untamed,

Men are restrained,

Consider themselves as the epitome of strength!

Emotions are flawed,

And tenderness feminine,

Masochism is the motto of life!

I wonder who will change this toxicity of minds?

Maybe the one who makes us believe that men understand!

Be it a father, a husband, a friend, who performs one's duties as best as one can!

When love is unconditional, and friendship a beautiful art!

When there are no expectations, only unconditional support, no questions asked!

I look forward to the day this dream would come true!

That would be the day we get a glimpse of heaven too!

Her

Purple lips and rainbow hair,
People mock her but she doesn't care!

Scars and bruises cover her face,
People pity her unaware of her fame!

Dressed in pantsuits, with sneakers on her feet,
She marches on towards pinnacles nonchalantly!

She lives in a war zone everyday,
Diatribes hurting her worse than a bullet!

But what makes her special are you aware?
It is her smile that hides all the pain!

She buries her sorrows deep inside her heart,
And lives her life the way that she wants!

She breaks all the stereotypes you throw her way,
She has now learnt how to make her own way the hard way!

3. DISCOVERING THE UNTHOUGHT

There have been two occasions over the years where I have tried to write something different from my usual style. Once it was a haiku and trust me when I learnt the definition of one, I was more than confused. How do you even express with restrictions? Isn't poetry supposed to be liberating? But although it was frustrating in the beginning, the ending was pretty alright because this poem made it into a list of good Haikus on Wattpad.

In the second instance, I was supposed to write a four-lined poem on Gandhiji. My dilemma was probably longer than the poem in its entirety. How do you describe a man badged with accomplishments in mere four lines, but the attempt was successful as it won me a college poem competition.

Now that I am done bragging, lets dive into the shortest section of this book, Discovering the Unthought.

Haiku

Waves crashing the shore,
White pebbles lie in my hands,
But only in dreams!

Gandhiji

Non-violence and peace were his aphorisms,
But the insurgents killed the father cause he was independent!
Science says energy gets absorbed and it did,
Gandhiji conquered our hearts while the rebels and their
pessimistic vibes are long forgotten!

4. DECLARATIONS OF LOVE

Endings always come quicker than anticipated, so here we are at the very last section of this book. I still remember how I started writing poems. It was one fine birthday of my mother where I had made her yet again a horrible greeting card because sadly my drawing and painting skills have never emerged from the seeds. It was on this occasion that my mother encouraged me to divert my interests from drawing to expressing my feelings in words. This is how from class 6, I have been writing poems for my loved ones on their special occasions. While I can't publish all the poems here, let me take you through a few of my works portraying my love for the jewels of my life.
Presenting to you the very last section of this book, Declarations of Love.

Dear Papa

I smiled when I first saw, you told me one day,
You still manage to make me smile even when I am enervated!

Soul so magnanimous, you bolster me in everyway,
You are never odious, an anomaly for this age!

Holding my little fingers, you taught me how to walk,
You make me feel placid enough to share with you all my
thoughts!

You made maths fun when I was in school,
Sat with me night after night while I studied, keeping me awake
with your humour tools!

Oh, how lucky I am to have a father like you,
You are exemplary, no one can be like you!

Dear Mom

I want someone to love me, dear God,
Someone to guide me everytime I am lost!

Someone to listen to my gibberish with a smile,
Someone who looks at me as if I were their life!

Someone who teaches me the ropes of this world,
Someone who keeps me safe from the scary creatures nocturnal!

Someone who defends me from the trolls,
Someone who can read the thoughts of my soul!

Someone who has faith in everything I do,
Someone I can depend on anytime I need someone to turn to!

'Oh child!', the God said, 'there's no one but one who fits the role!'
' I bless you with a mother to behold!'

The First Man I have ever Loved

The moon hung in the sky,
Feeling lonely and a little shy!

She had no friends, no siblings, no relatives,
Her existence for her was a phenomenon enigmatic!

Rocky body, greyish shade,
She wasn't blessed like her contemporaries in the Milky Way!

Earth was a beauty with a rainbow of colours, Mars was red like its spirited nature!

Jupiter was huge and had a bunch of friends roaming around it,
Saturn had rings icy and aphrodisiac!

Self-pity bloomed within her heart,
And a lonely tear escaped like a traitor falling on the Earth!

Afraid of the consequences she closed her eyes,
When she heard his raspy voice!

' Don't you cry my dear child, I will be your friend and guide!'

From that day on a new era began,
The moon started revolving around the Earth, becoming an exemplary beauty for the humans born there!

You are my Earth, my support structure,
The best father in the world unquestioned!

My Inspiration

Every night I search for the brightest star in the sky for I know it would be you,
Sparkling away for the ones who live in a gloomy dark world and being their muse!

Everytime I am in trouble all I remember is you,
For I know if guardians angels exist, mine is forever going to be you!

How is it that despite having never met, I miss you so much?
Maybe it's the stories about your marvelous persona and courage that always leave a mark on me inspiring me to do better!

You don't need to meet someone to know them is all I know,
For I can feel your presence always guiding me towards the path of goodness and hope!

Mumma says that we are similar in many ways, I am like you,
Never have I been more proud to be compared to someone I never knew!

You have lived on in all our hearts each and every day,
Love conquering the fact that we only get to see through the eyes of heart and memories stored away in our brains!

Epiphany

'Happiness is a luxury not everyone gets it', someone said,
'But what indeed is happiness', I retorted back in dismay!

'Is happiness money or is it pride or is it like a rare blue diamond',
I asked,
'It's a feeling', my mind replied and so did the person who made
the remark!

'A feeling', I mocked, 'a feeling you say is ardous?',
'It's not the feeling that's onerous, it's the possibility of feeling
happy that's like gold dust!'

'Who, who said that I screamed!',
For there was no one apart from the arrogant man present there
and me.

The old wise tree opened its eyes, and looked at me with a
knowing smile,
I swayed a bit from the shock, while the man fainted and the tree
just looked on wondering maybe at my lack of manners or just
thinking I am naive!

'Greetings Mr Tree', I said with a trembling voice,
The tree shook with laughter, finding joy in my fright!

'My dear girl', the tree said now with a serious tone,
'Do you know why you feel like what the man said is a myth?'
I shook my head briskly, unable to formulate words for I felt like I was paralyzed at my limbs!

'You are fortunate to have a father who is kind, who makes you laugh and who always takes care of you', it said, 'he is the reason for your beliefs and good mental health!'
Now I realize what a treasure I possess, my father is the reason why happiness is the gold dust that I already possess!

Silver Jubilee of Love

A beauty in a purple suit,
Stole his heart away,
He looked at her and thanked God for giving him his soulmate!

Eyes cast down, all she could think of was the pattern of his shirt,
A little shy, a little hesitant, she couldn't utter a word,
Hiding behind her mother, she finally looked at him,
Is he really the one was all she could think!

The day of their marriage finally arrived,
The Prince and the Princess vowed to always be by each other's side,
The magic of love sparkles through good people they say and it did,
Through ups and downs, their bond became diamond-
Two people, transitioned into one soul that always outshines the world's evils!

Love is friendship is what I heard in movies,
But love is also honesty, respect and trust is what I have learnt from them!

No one like You

Four and half hours or five and a half,
You stayed up to guard me from fears
aghast!

Four and half hours or five and a half,
You encouraged me when I felt torn apart!

Four and half hours or five and a half,
You listened to me blabber irrelevant bruits!

Four and half hours or five and a half,
You were there for me when no one
could!

You inspire me by being you everyday,
Selfless, loving and perfect in all ways!

Reminiscing

A tiny finger held in a large warm hand,
A large beam on both the faces, as they moved through mysterious lands!

A bag full of chocolates, and a car smelling like fuel,
A tune on the radio that they both didn't find so cool!

A stop for some cold drinks,
A stop for some work!

A stop to cherish all the memories that were stored that day in the brain's reserves!
Little by little she extracts those treasures that were buried long ago,
And every bit leaves her craving for more!

How would life be if she didn't have him as her friend?
She can't fathom to think of a journey without this marvellous man!

Because of You

Watching you watch me even when I am not in sight,
Listening to you talking when panic keeps me up at night!

Laughing with you unexpectedly when atrocities strike,
Crying in front of you when destiny plays with my psyche!

Like a mirror you show me my true- self everyday,
Like the North star you guide me when I run towards a mirage on
a sunny desert lane !

You are my sun, and I a mere planet orbitting your eminence,
I am cause you are, else I am nothing but an insignificant atom in
a wide wide space!

Angel

Like the flowers in the fields of Elysium,
You spread your fragrance far and wide!

Drifting slowly like a gentle breeze amidst pandemonium,
You touch every soul with your empathetic smile!

Like Elpis in the jar of Pandora,
You stay behind countless times-
Always working from the shadows-
You never look for a prize!

Love abundant like cornucopia,
Your affection only grows,
What would I be without you is all I think with my brows
furrowed!

Other Works

Thoughts in my Mind has ended here but here's a list of some other works from me that aren't poetry. Some of my novels:

- That Night At The Hotel
- Lost Stars
- Selina(Coming out this December)
- Rosa, the sequel to Selina is coming soon to your favorite stores!

Follow my Instagram(@somyasworld) to stay updated.

Note: All my books are available now on Amazon, Flipkart(India), Barnes and Noble and Notion Press apart from 30000+ other platforms

www.ingramcontent.com/pod-product-compliance
Lightning Source LLC
LaVergne TN
LVHW090139160826
845673LV00017B/2522

* 9 7 9 8 8 9 1 8 6 6 3 0 0 *